United States Government Accountability Office

Report to the Ranking Member, Subcommittee on Environment and the Economy, Committee on Energy and Commerce, House of Representatives

August 2013

PESTICIDES

I0448370

EPA Should Take Steps to Improve Its Oversight of Conditional Registrations

August 2013

GAO Highlights

Highlights of GAO-13-145, a report to the Ranking Member, Subcommittee on Environment and the Economy, Committee on Energy and Commerce, House of Representatives

PESTICIDES

EPA Should Take Steps to Improve Its Oversight of Conditional Registrations

Why GAO Did This Study

As of September 2010, more than 16,000 pesticides were registered for use in the United States, according to EPA. EPA reviews health and environmental effects data submitted by a company and may register a pesticide or, alternatively, grant a "conditional registration" for a pesticide under certain circumstances, even though some of the required data may not have been submitted or reviewed. The company must provide the missing data within a specified time. In 2010, environmental and other groups charged that EPA had overused conditional registrations and did not appear to have a reliable system to identify whether the required data had been submitted. GAO was asked to examine issues related to EPA's use of conditional registrations for pesticides. This report examines the (1) number of conditional registrations EPA has granted and the basis for these, (2) extent to which EPA ensures that companies submit the required additional data and EPA reviews the data, and (3) views of relevant stakeholders on EPA's use of conditional registrations. GAO reviewed EPA data and surveyed stakeholders, among other things.

What GAO Recommends

GAO recommends, in part, that EPA consider and implement options for an automated system to better track conditional registrations. EPA agreed with GAO's recommendations and noted specific actions it will take to implement them.

View GAO-13-145. For more information, contact J. Alfredo Gómez, (202) 512-3841 or gomezj@gao.gov.

What GAO Found

The total number of conditional registrations granted is unclear, as the Environmental Protection Agency (EPA) reports that its data are inaccurate for several reasons. First, the database used to track conditional registrations does not allow officials to change a pesticide's registration status from conditional to unconditional once the registrant has satisfied all requirements, thereby overstating the number of conditional registrations. Second, EPA staff have misused the term "conditional registration," incorrectly classifying pesticide registrations as conditional when, for example, they require a label change, which is not a basis in statute for a conditional registration. According to EPA documents and officials, weaknesses in guidance and training, management oversight, and data management contributed to these misclassification problems. For example, according to EPA documents, there was limited, organized management oversight to ensure that regulatory actions were not misclassified as conditional registrations. As of July 2013, EPA officials told GAO that the agency has taken or is planning to take several actions to more accurately account for conditional registrations, including beginning to design a new automated data system to more accurately track conditional registrations.

The extent to which EPA ensures that companies submit additional required data and EPA reviews these data is unknown. Specifically, EPA does not have a reliable system, such as an automated data system, to track key information related to conditional registrations, including whether companies have submitted additional data within required time frames. As a result, pesticides with conditional registrations could be marketed for years without EPA's receipt and review of these data. In the absence of a reliable system for managing conditional registrations, EPA relies on a variety of routine program operations, such as its review of a company's changes to a pesticide registration, to discover that data are missing. However, these methods fall short of what is needed because they are neither comprehensive nor do they ensure timely submission of these data. According to federal internal control standards, EPA's lack of a reliable system for managing conditional registrations constitutes an internal control weakness because the agency lacks an effective mechanism for program oversight and decision making.

Stakeholders GAO surveyed—representatives of consumer, environmental, industry, legal, producer, science, and state government groups—generally said EPA needs to improve its conditional registration process. For example, some stated EPA should improve its data systems for tracking conditional registrations to ensure that required data are submitted and reviewed in a timely manner. However, stakeholder views varied on the benefits and disadvantages of conditionally registering pesticides. For example, some consumer, industry, legal, producer, and state government stakeholders stated that the conditional registration process promotes innovation by bringing new technologies to the marketplace more quickly. In contrast, some consumer, environmental, legal, science, and state government stakeholders voiced concerns that conditional registration allows products with safety that has not been fully evaluated into the marketplace.

_____ **United States Government Accountability Office**

Contents

Abbreviations

DCI	Data Call-In
EPA	Environmental Protection Agency
FIFRA	Federal Insecticide, Fungicide, and Rodenticide Act
FFDCA	Federal Food, Drug, and Cosmetic Act
NRDC	Natural Resources Defense Council
OMB	Office of Management and Budget
OPP	Office of Pesticide Programs
OPPIN	Office of Pesticide Programs Information Network
PRIA	Pesticide Registration Improvement Act of 2003
PRISM	Pesticide Registration Information System

GAO U.S. GOVERNMENT ACCOUNTABILITY OFFICE

441 G St. N.W.
Washington, DC 20548

August 8, 2013

The Honorable Paul D. Tonko
Ranking Member
Subcommittee on Environment and the Economy
Committee on Energy and Commerce
House of Representatives

Dear Mr. Tonko:

As of September 2010, more than 16,000 pesticides were registered for use in the United States, according to the Environmental Protection Agency (EPA). In addition, expenditures for pesticides—primarily for use in agriculture—totaled $12.5 billion in 2007, the latest year for which data are available from EPA. These pesticides—chemicals or biological substances used to destroy or control weeds or unwanted insects, fungi, rodents, bacteria and other pests—contribute significantly to agricultural productivity by preventing crop damage and improving public health by controlling disease-carrying pests. However, if used improperly, pesticides may adversely affect human health by, for example, increasing the risk of cancer and neurological disorders caused by pesticide residues on food crops. Pesticides may also damage the environment by, for example, killing or causing reproductive abnormalities in species other than those which the pesticide is intended to kill, including fish, birds, and other wildlife.

Under the Federal Insecticide, Fungicide, and Rodenticide Act, as amended, (FIFRA),[1] EPA registers pesticides distributed, sold, or used in the United States and prescribes labeling and other regulatory requirements to prevent unreasonable adverse effects on the environment.[2] To obtain a registration, a company or person (registrant)

---

[1] Act of June 25, 1947, ch. 125, 61 Stat. 163 (codified as amended at 7 U.S.C. §§ 136-136y).

[2] The phrase "unreasonable adverse effects on the environment" is defined in FIFRA, in part, to mean (1) any unreasonable risk to man or the environment, taking into account the economic, social, and environmental costs and benefits of the use of any pesticide, or (2) a human dietary risk from residues that result from a use of a pesticide in or on any food inconsistent with the standard for tolerance under section 408 of the Federal Food, Drug, and Cosmetic Act, 21 U.S.C.§ 346a. This standard requires EPA to consider both the benefits and risks of using a pesticide.

is to submit an application containing health and environmental effects data and other information on a pesticide for EPA's review.[3] After reviewing the information, in general, EPA may (1) register the pesticide and set a tolerance level (i.e., the maximum pesticide residue allowed) for those pesticides used on food or animal feed,[4] (2) notify the registrant of deficiencies in the data or the need for additional information, or (3) deny the application.

FIFRA section 3(c)(5) and section 3(c)(7) set forth two sets of statutory standards under which EPA may register pesticides. EPA is authorized to grant registrations under section 3(c)(5) if EPA determines, among other things, that the application materials provided satisfy the requirements of the statutes and that the information those materials contain concerning the pesticide demonstrates that, when used in accordance with widespread and commonly recognized practice, the product will not generally cause unreasonable adverse effects on the environment. Such registrations are commonly referred to as "unconditional" registrations because they are approved without EPA imposing a requirement on the registrant to develop additional data.

In addition, section 3(c)(7) of FIFRA provides EPA the authority to grant a "conditional registration" for a pesticide product under certain circumstances, although some necessary data have not been provided by the registrant in the application. Under this authority, EPA may grant a conditional registration for pesticide products that are identical or substantially similar to pesticide products that are already registered or for a new use of a currently registered product as long as EPA determines, among other things, that the pesticide will not significantly increase the risk of unreasonable adverse effects on the environment. This authority also allows EPA to grant a conditional registration for pesticide products with new active ingredients where data are missing from the application because the requirement for the data was imposed so recently that the registrant did not have adequate time to generate the data and EPA

---

[3]According to Office of Pesticide Programs (OPP) officials, applicants for pesticide registrations are usually pesticide product manufacturers. When EPA registers an applicant's pesticide product, the applicant is then called a registrant. For the purposes of this report, we refer to applicants as registrants.

[4]Under the Federal Food, Drug, and Cosmetic Act, EPA is authorized to establish tolerances—or exemptions for the requirement of a tolerance—for pesticide residues that remain in food or animal feed.

GAO-13-145 Conditional Pesticide Registration

determines, among other things, that the pesticide will not cause unreasonable adverse effects on the environment during the time needed to generate the data.[5] According to EPA officials, registrants typically have from 1 to 4 years to provide the missing data required by a conditional registration.

In 2010, an environmental group questioned EPA's use of conditional registrations in the pesticide program, and other consumer and science groups supported this position. The environmental group charged that EPA had overused conditional registrations, stating that information from EPA's Office of Pesticide Programs Information Network (OPPIN) data system showed that conditional registrations represented the majority of active registrations.[6] The group also pointed out that the OPPIN data indicated that some pesticide products had been conditionally registered for 20 years or more.

In this context, you asked us to examine EPA's procedures for granting conditional registrations. Accordingly, we examined the (1) number of conditional pesticide registrations EPA has granted and the basis for granting these registrations; (2) extent to which EPA ensures that registrants submit the additional data required as part of conditional registrations and reviews these data; and (3) views of relevant stakeholders on EPA's use of conditional registrations, including ways, if any, to improve the conditional registration process.

To address these objectives, we reviewed relevant federal statutes and regulations, EPA guidance documents and internal reviews, federal internal control standards, and previous GAO and EPA Inspector General reports.[7] We also requested that EPA's Office of Pesticide Programs (OPP) provide summary data on its issuance of conditional registrations, including (1) the number of pesticide registrations currently in conditional

---

[5]An active ingredient is the chemical or substance component of a pesticide product that will prevent, destroy, repel, or mitigate a pest.

[6]EPA refers to registrations that are in effect (i.e., the registration has not been suspended or canceled) as "active" registrations. For purposes of this report, unless otherwise indicated, all registrations discussed are "active."

[7]EPA Office of Inspector General, *EPA's Pesticide Program*, Report no. E1EPE2-05-0015-4100205, Mar. 11, 1994; EPA Office of Inspector General, *Pesticides: Follow-up Report on EPA's Pesticide Program*, Report no. 00P00011, March 27, 2000. GAO reports are listed under "Related GAO Products" at the end of this report.

status and how long they have been in this status; (2) the total number of current pesticide registrations (conditional and unconditional); and (3) for fiscal years 1997 through 2011, the number of conditional registrations granted for each year and the basis on which these were granted (i.e., identical/substantially similar pesticides, new uses, or new active ingredients). In addition, we asked OPP to provide information on the number of pesticides that (1) have a conditional registration, but the registrant has not submitted the additional required data by the specified due date; (2) have a conditional registration and the registrant has submitted the additional required data, but EPA has not reviewed these data; (3) still have a conditional registration, even though the registrant has submitted, and EPA has reviewed, the additional required data; and (4) had been changed from conditional to unconditional status. However, after interviewing OPP officials and reviewing past GAO, Inspector General, and EPA contractor studies examining OPP's data management, especially its use of OPPIN, we concluded that EPA could not provide us with sufficiently reliable data for obtaining summary level information on conditional pesticide registrations. In the absence of these data, we discussed with OPP officials the data limitations they face using OPPIN and any potential workarounds they employ or are planning. In addition, we interviewed OPP officials and reviewed documentation they provided to obtain further information and clarification on EPA's conditional registration process, including any planned responses to internal review or external stakeholder concerns. To obtain the views of relevant stakeholders on EPA's conditional registration process and ways, if any, to improve it, we used the results of a literature search and other sources to develop a list of consumer, environmental, industry, legal, producer, science, and state government stakeholders. From this list, we selected a nonprobability sample of stakeholders from each category to contact, for a total of 35 stakeholders.[8] We then developed, pretested, and e-mailed a questionnaire to obtain these stakeholders' views. Twenty-four out of 35 stakeholders provided responses to our questionnaire. We performed a content analysis of the questionnaire responses to identify common themes regarding stakeholders' views on

[8]Because this was a nonprobability sample, the information collected in response to the questionnaire about EPA's use of conditional registrations cannot be generalized to all consumer, environmental, industry, legal, producer, science, and state government stakeholders but provides illustrative information on the views of such stakeholders by category.

EPA's use of conditional registrations. Appendix I provides a more detailed description of our objectives, scope, and methodology.

We conducted this performance audit from September 2011 to August 2013 in accordance with generally accepted government auditing standards. Those standards require that we plan and perform the audit to obtain sufficient, appropriate evidence to provide a reasonable basis for our findings and conclusions based on our audit objectives. We believe that the evidence obtained provides a reasonable basis for our findings and conclusions based on our audit objectives.

Background

The primary federal laws that govern how EPA regulates pesticides in the United States are FIFRA and the Federal Food, Drug, and Cosmetic Act (FFDCA).[9] Under FIFRA implementing regulations,[10] EPA is to review applications for pesticide products and register those that it determines will meet the FIFRA statutory standards for registration. If the use of a pesticide would result in a residue of the substance in or on food or animal feed, EPA may not register a pesticide under FIFRA unless it can determine that the residue is "safe" as defined by FFDCA. Under FFDCA, safe means that EPA has determined, among other things, that there is a reasonable certainty that no harm will result from aggregate exposure to the pesticide residue, including all anticipated dietary exposures and all other nonoccupational exposures for which there is reliable information.[11] EPA may establish a tolerance level—the maximum permissible pesticide residue in or on food or animal feed that is sold—that meets the FFDCA safety standard or may choose to grant an exemption for a tolerance.[12]

---

[9]21 U.S.C. §§ 301-399f.

[10]40 C.F.R. pts. 152-180.

[11]Nonoccupational exposures are those experienced by the general population, as opposed to those experienced by specific groups of pesticide users, such as farm workers and pest control operators.

[12]To make the safety finding, EPA considers, among other things, the toxicity of the pesticide and its breakdown products, aggregate exposure to the pesticide in foods and from other nonoccupational sources of exposure, and any special risks posed to infants and children. EPA may grant an exemption from the requirement to have a tolerance when there is a reasonable certainty that no harm will result from aggregate exposure, including all anticipated dietary exposures for which there is reliable information.

OPP—the EPA office primarily responsible for regulating the use of pesticides—has regulatory staff in three divisions—Registration, Biopesticides and Pollution Prevention, and Antimicrobials—that are responsible for registering pesticides.[13] The registration process formally begins when a registrant submits an application to OPP for a particular pesticide. This application is to include data to support the registration of the pesticide. In reviewing the application, OPP is to examine, among other things, the pesticide's ingredients; the site or crop on which it is to be used; the amount, frequency, and timing of its use; and storage and disposal practices. OPP is also to review toxicity tests and studies showing how the pesticide affects human health and the environment. According to OPP officials, the length of time OPP takes from the initial review of an application to the final decision on whether to register a pesticide depends on many factors—including whether the pesticide being reviewed is similar to any pesticide EPA has previously reviewed—and, according to OPP officials, can take from 3 to 24 months. After OPP completes its review and approves the submitted package, EPA may register the pesticide without imposing requirements for additional data (unconditional registration) under FIFRA 3(c)(5) if EPA determines, among other things, that use of the pesticide in accordance with label directions will not have unreasonable adverse effects on the environment.[14]

---

[13]The Registration Division is responsible for certain regulatory activities related to market entry of new pesticides—including product registrations, amendments, tolerances, experimental use permits, and emergency exemptions—associated with conventional pesticides, which are man-made chemicals developed and produced primarily or only for use as pesticides. The Biopesticides and Pollution Prevention Division is responsible for all regulatory activities associated with biologically based pesticides, which are chemicals derived from plants, fungi, bacteria or other natural substances that can be used for pest control, as well as for Plant-Incorporated Protectants, which refers to the material added to or generated in plants that have been genetically engineered to express a pesticidal property. The Antimicrobials Division is responsible for all regulatory activities associated with antimicrobial pesticides, which are chemical substances that can be used to kill microorganisms.

[14]FIFRA section 3(c)(5) provides that the EPA Administrator shall register a pesticide if the Administrator determines, among other things, that (1) the pesticide's composition is such as to warrant the proposed claims for it; (2) its labeling and other material required to be submitted comply with the requirements of FIFRA; (3) it will perform its intended function without unreasonable adverse effects on the environment; and (4) when used in accordance with widespread and commonly recognized practice it will not generally cause unreasonable adverse effects on the environment.

Alternatively, FIFRA section 3(c)(7) allows EPA to grant a conditional registration for pesticides in the following circumstances:

- *Identical/substantially similar pesticides (FIFRA Section 3(c)(7)(A)).* EPA may conditionally approve an application for registration or an amended registration for a pesticide product if the agency determines that

  - the pesticide and proposed use are identical or substantially similar to any currently registered pesticide and its uses, or differ only in ways that will not significantly increase the risk of unreasonable adverse effects on the environment; and

  - approving the registration or amendment in the manner proposed would not significantly increase the risk of any unreasonable adverse effect on the environment.

Each registration issued under 3(c)(7)(A) must submit or cite the same data that would be required for the unconditional registration of a similar product.

- *New uses (FIFRA Section 3(c)(7)(B)).* A current pesticide registration may be amended to allow additional uses, even if the data concerning the pesticide may be insufficient to support unconditional registration, if EPA determines that

  - the applicant has submitted satisfactory data pertaining to the proposed additional use; and

  - amending the registration would not significantly increase the risk of unreasonable adverse effect on the environment.

Each registrant must submit or cite the same data that would be required for the unconditional registration of a similar product.[15]

- *New active ingredients (FIFRA Section 3(c)(7)(C)).* A pesticide containing a new active ingredient not found in any currently registered pesticide can be conditionally registered for a period reasonably sufficient for the generation and submission of required data, if EPA determines

  - insufficient time has elapsed since the imposition of the data requirement for those data to be developed and on the condition that when the agency receives such data that they do not meet or exceed risk criteria stated in the regulations issued under FIFRA and other conditions issued by the agency;

  - the use of the pesticide during the period of the conditional registration will not cause unreasonable adverse effect on the environment; and

  - the use of the pesticide is in the public interest.

After a pesticide product is conditionally registered under FIFRA section (3)(c)(7), the registrant receives a notice indicating the terms of the conditional registration, including a list of any additional data that will need to be submitted and deadlines for submitting these data. Figure 1 summarizes the pesticide registration and tolerance setting process.

---

[15]In addition, FIFRA implementing regulations state that EPA will not approve the conditional registration of a pesticide product for a new use if (1) the pesticide is the subject of a special review to determine if the use of the pesticide may result in unreasonable adverse effects based on a use of the product that results in human dietary exposure or (2) the proposed new use is for a major food or feed crop (such as corn or soy beans), or involves use on a minor food (including many fruits and vegetables) or feed crop for which there is an effective alternative registered pesticide that does not meet the FIFRA criteria for risk associated with human dietary exposure.

Figure 1: General Overview of EPA Pesticide Registration and Tolerance Setting Process

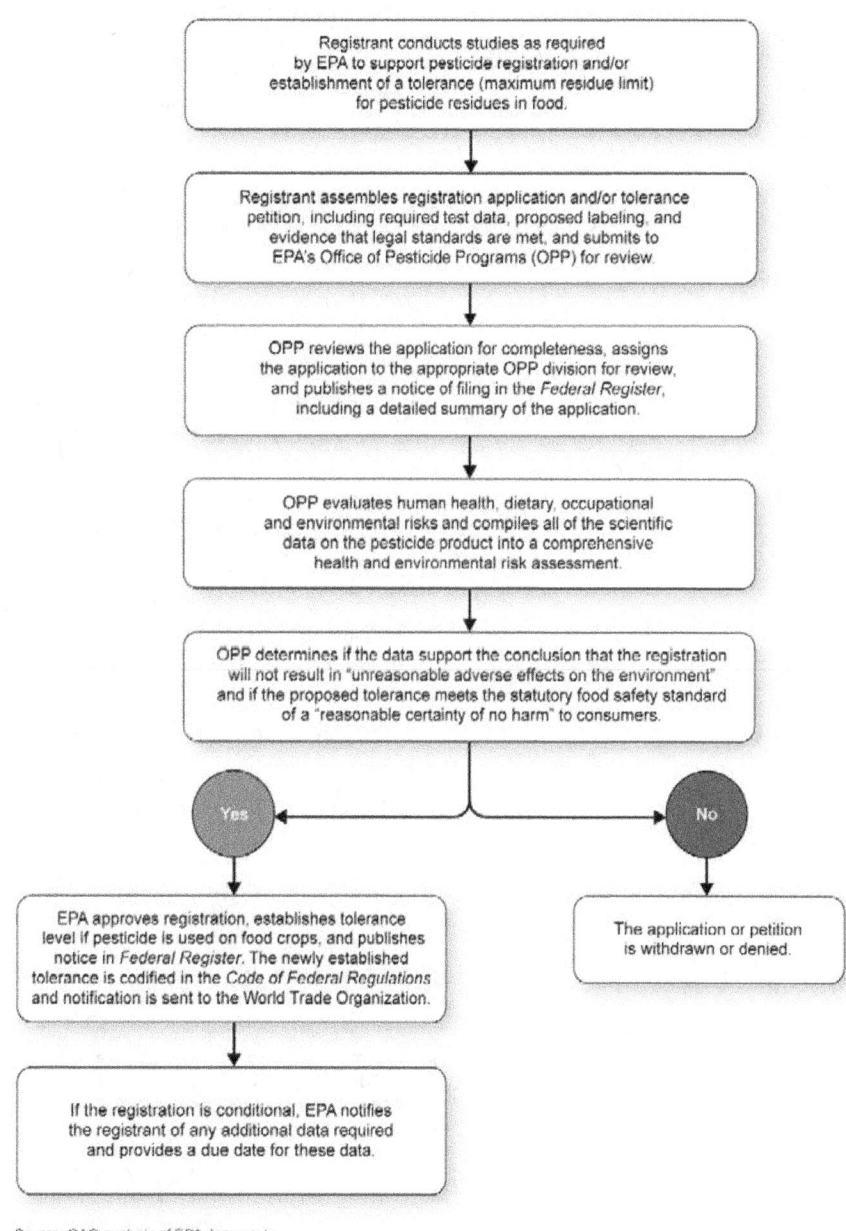

Source: GAO analysis of EPA documents.

GAO-13-145 Conditional Pesticide Registration

According to EPA officials, once a pesticide is conditionally registered, EPA typically grants a period of time, generally 1 to 4 years, for the registrant to provide the required data. The registrant can ask EPA to waive the requirement for additional information or, according to EPA officials, extend the time frame. If the registrant does not submit the data specified within the required time frame, EPA can cancel the pesticide registration.

Before a pesticide can be sold or distributed in the United States, it must be registered under FIFRA.[16] At any time, EPA may initiate a suspension or cancellation proceeding for a pesticide registration if safety concerns develop. For example, EPA began proceedings to cancel some uses of Carbofuran[17]—an insecticide and nematicide that was registered to control pests in soils and on leaves in a variety of field, fruit, and vegetable crops—after the agency determined that the dietary, worker, and ecological risks of this pesticide were unacceptable.[18]

Another check on the safety of registered pesticide products is the requirement in FIFRA section 6(a)(2) and FIFRA implementing regulations that registrants report adverse effects-related information to EPA. For example, registrants are required to submit certain toxicity information concerning the product both before and after registration, such as information on the product's toxicity to nontarget plant species.

In addition, as required by FIFRA,[19] EPA is to review the safety of each registered pesticide every 15 years to help ensure that each pesticide registration continues to satisfy the regulatory standard. In 2007, EPA

---

[16]In addition to an EPA registration, registrants must also comply with state regulations, some of which require registration in the state before the product can be sold or distributed in that state.

[17]74 Fed. Reg. 11,551 (Mar. 18, 2009).

[18]A nematicide kills nematodes, which are microscopic, worm-like organisms that feed on plant roots.

[19]FIFRA section 3(g) requires that EPA periodically reevaluate registered pesticides.

began conducting these reviews under its registration review program.[20] As a part of this program, if EPA determines that additional data are needed to support the continued registration of a pesticide, the agency may issue a Data Call-In (DCI) notice, as authorized by FIFRA section 3(c)(2)(B), requiring the registrant to provide the data by a specific date. Also, at any time after a pesticide is registered, a registrant may apply to amend the registration and, according to OPP officials, such requests are reviewed as though the registrant is seeking approval for a new pesticide. While reviewing such requests, the agency may also issue a DCI notice requiring the registrant to provide additional data by a specific date. If a registrant fails to provide the data requested through a DCI, EPA may suspend the pesticide's registration under authority of FIFRA section 3(c)(2)(B).

In 2003 amendments to FIFRA,[21] pesticide registration fees paid by registrants were established for some registration actions, such as registrations for new uses of pesticides, to help pay for registration costs. Earlier amendments to FIFRA, enacted in 1988, established annual registration maintenance fees—fees used to support the review of existing pesticide registrations. For fiscal year 2012, EPA reported that it collected a total of $37.6 million from fees, including $22 million in maintenance fees.[22]

In July 2010, an environmental group requested information from EPA regarding conditional registrations, including the number of conditional

---

[20]Procedural regulations for the registration review of pesticides became effective on October 10, 2006. By law, the agency must complete the first 15-year cycle of registration review by October 1, 2022. The agency must complete the registration review of each new pesticide active ingredient within 15 years of its initial registration. Previously, EPA conducted similar reviews of pesticides first registered before November 1984 under its reregistration program. Registration review is replacing the reregistration program. Unlike reregistration, registration review is to operate continuously and encompass all registered pesticides, according to EPA.

[21]The Pesticide Registration Improvement Act of 2003 (PRIA), Pub. L. No. 108-199, Div. G, Tit. V, § 501, 118 Stat. 419 (2004), amended FIFRA by, among other things, establishing pesticide registration fees for some registration actions. PRIA was reauthorized in 2007 (Pesticide Registration Improvement Renewal Act of 2007, Pub. L. No. 110-94, 121 Stat. 1000 (2007) or PRIA 2) and again in 2012 (Pesticide Registration Improvement Extension Act of 2012, Pub. L. No. 112-177, 126 Stat. 1327, or PRIA 3).

[22]EPA, *Fiscal Year 2012 Justification of Appropriation Estimates for the Committee on Appropriations,* EPA-190-R-11-003.

GAO-13-145 Conditional Pesticide Registration

registrations the agency had issued, whether registrants had submitted the additional data required by the registrations, and whether EPA had reviewed the data submitted.[23] OPP provided the group with information from the OPPIN data system on the number of pesticide registrations that had been categorized as conditional. Subsequently, in September 2010, the environmental group raised concerns about EPA's use of its conditional registration authority, and several other environmental groups and other interested parties supported this position. Among other things, the environmental group asserted that EPA had overused conditional registrations and did not appear to have a reliable tracking system to identify the status of conditionally registered pesticides to ensure that registrants submitted, and EPA reviewed, additional data in a timely manner.[24] In addition, the group noted that the information EPA provided indicated that many pesticides have remained in conditional status for many years. For example, the information showed that over 3,200 pesticides had been in conditional status since 1995 (15 years) and that 2,100 pesticides had been in conditional status since 1990 (20 years).

Total Number of Conditional Registrations Granted Is Unclear, as EPA Found Data to Be Inaccurate

The number of active conditional registrations EPA has granted is unclear, according to OPP officials who, as a result of a 2011 EPA review, found the agency's registration data to be inaccurate and the basis for granting some of these registrations to be inappropriately classified. Specifically, an internal review of OPP's conditional registration program found that OPPIN does not allow officials to change a pesticide's registration status from conditional to unconditional once the registrant has satisfied all data requirements, and the basis for many registration decisions was mischaracterized as conditional. In addition, based on the internal review, OPP officials concluded that several weaknesses contributed to this misclassification problem, including insufficient guidance and training, management oversight, and data management. As of July 2013, OPP officials told us that the office has taken or is planning to take several actions to more accurately account for conditional registrations.

---

[23]The Natural Resources Defense Council (NRDC) requested the information regarding EPA's use of conditional registrations.

[24]The groups that concurred with NRDC's position on EPA's use of conditional registrations were Alaska Community Action on Toxics, Beyond Pesticides, Center for Environmental Health, Friends of the Earth U.S., Organic Consumers Association, Pesticide Action Network North America, and TEDX The Endocrine Disruptor Exchange.

EPA Found Conditional Registration Data to Be Inaccurate and That the Basis for Many Registrations Was Inappropriately Classified

According to OPP officials, following an internal review of its conditional registration program that it completed in March 2011, OPP concluded that the OPPIN data on the number of conditional registrations were inaccurate. The internal review was conducted, in part, to determine the number of conditional registrations granted by EPA. According to information on OPP's website,[25] during the internal review, OPP determined that OPPIN contained 16,156 active pesticide registrations and that 11,205 (69 percent) of these pesticides were conditionally registered. However, OPP officials concluded, based on the internal review, that the data were inaccurate, and that the number of conditional registrations was overstated, for two reasons. First, once a registration is classified as conditional in OPPIN, its status in this data system cannot be changed from conditional to unconditional, when, for example, the registrant has satisfied all data requirements imposed. According to the internal review, OPPIN is an older system that was not designed specifically to track conditional registrations and thus is ill-suited for that purpose. To determine the current number of conditionally registered pesticides, OPP officials said detailed paper files that support each pesticide registration would need to be reviewed, which would be a very time-consuming process. OPP officials indicated that they plan to develop a new automated system for tracking conditional registrations and, in fiscal year 2013, they began using a portion of the registration maintenance fees collected annually to begin exploring the feasibility of implementing such a system.[26] However, these officials were uncertain about the ultimate cost of this system, what sources they would use for any additional funding, and when the system would be operational.

Second, as a result of the internal review, OPP found that its regulatory staff had incorrectly categorized the basis for many program actions in OPPIN as "conditional registrations" and that these incorrect

---

[25]OPP's website can be found at http://www.epa.gov/pesticides/regulating/conditional-registration.html.

[26]The Pesticide Registration Improvement Extension Act of 2012 amended FIFRA to provide, among other things, funding to improve the information systems capabilities for OPP; the amendments provide that this funding is to support enhancing the systems capacity to track pesticide registration decisions, including the status of conditional registrations. The amendments authorize $800,000 per year for 5 years to be set aside from the maintenance fees to fund these enhancements, including those related to conditional registrations. In addition, the amendments require, in part, that EPA report each year through 2017 on its progress in implementing a system for tracking the status of conditional registrations.

categorizations resulted in an overcounting of conditional registrations. According to the internal review, OPP staff had used conditional registrations to describe a variety of actions that fall outside of the circumstances authorized by FIFRA Section 3(c)(7). For example, according to OPP officials and the internal review, OPP staff had assigned the category "conditional registration" to situations where approval of a registration is contingent upon the "condition" that the registrant makes a change that does not involve generating additional data. These situations included certain changes to pesticide product labels—such as strengthening precautionary statements—that are not specified by FIFRA section 3(c)(7), according to the results of the internal review. Similarly, OPP staff categorized as "conditional registrations" situations where the agency requested registrants to provide certain pesticide product-specific information—such as product chemistry studies related to storage stability that are used to determine label requirements—that do not fall under FIFRA Section 3(c)(7). The incorrect classification of actions as conditional registrations, according to the internal review, may leave the agency vulnerable to allegations by environmental, industry, and other stakeholders who assert that EPA inappropriately grants conditional registrations. However, according to OPP officials, all of the actions that were mistakenly categorized as conditional registrations were legitimate program actions that were lawful under other sections of FIFRA. We were unable to verify this assertion. Further, EPA still needs to take steps to correct these misclassifications in order to ensure the accuracy and integrity of its data and make clear the statutory basis for these program actions.

Several Weaknesses Contributed to Incorrect Data Entry on Conditional Registrations

Several weaknesses contributed to incorrect data entries into OPPIN. First, according to OPP officials, OPP regulatory staff did not have sufficient guidance or training to help them determine when a program action met the criteria for conditional registration. Second, according to OPP's internal review, there was limited, organized management oversight to ensure that regulatory actions not subject to the narrow scope of section 3(c)(7) were not mischaracterized by OPP staff as conditional registrations. As a result, as the internal review stated, the actions that were classified as conditional registrations have varied across OPP's three divisions and by individual entering data into OPPIN within each division. In addition, data management weaknesses contributed to the misclassification of registrations or other actions as conditional. For example, OPP officials said that OPPIN does not generate management reports of summary data that could have alerted managers to the excessive use of "conditional registration" due to the inaccurate classification of actions as conditional registrations by OPP staff. Under the federal standards for internal control, federal agencies are to employ internal control activities, such as management reviews at the functional or activity level, to help ensure that management's directives are carried out and to determine if agencies are effectively and efficiently using resources.[27] Without the ability to generate summary data on conditional registrations from OPPIN, OPP managers cannot easily conduct such reviews. However, they are still responsible for monitoring and ensuring the accuracy of conditional registration data.

In light of the apparent widespread misclassification of regulatory actions as conditional registration, OPP, as part of its internal review of conditional registrations, analyzed data in OPPIN to, among other things, determine EPA's historical use of conditional registrations, including how many of each of the three types of conditional registrations authorized by FIFRA section 3(c)(7) had been granted. The OPP official primarily responsible for conducting this analysis said the intent of the analysis was to show that (1) as noted on the OPP website, only a small portion of the conditional registrations granted by EPA were for new uses under section 3(c)(7)(B) or new active ingredients under section 3(c)(7)(C), as intended, and (2) most of the conditional registrations granted were for identical or substantially similar products under section 3(c)(7)(A). However, in reviewing this information and related documentation, we found that the information on the website was unclear, contained discrepancies, and used technical terms without defining them, which could lead to misinterpretation of the information. For example, the calculations presented on the website to support the conclusion that the overwhelming majority of actions identified in OPPIN as conditional registrations fall outside the circumstances authorized by FIFRA section 3(c)(7) incorrectly grouped conditional registrations for identical or substantially similar products authorized by section 3(c)(7)(A) with label amendments and other actions that fall outside the narrow scope of section 3(c)(7). After meeting with OPP officials in November 2012 to discuss the analysis, these officials acknowledged the website could be clearer and said that the website would be revised to clarify any confusing language and correct any inaccurate statements. However, OPP had no specific plan or

---

[27]GAO, *Standards for Internal Control in the Federal Government*, GAO/AIMD-00-21.3.1 (Washington, D.C.: November 1999).

time frame for doing so. As of July 2013, these clarifications and corrections had not been made.

OPP Is Taking, or Plans to Take, Actions to More Accurately Account for Conditional Registrations

Accurate and reliable data are essential to an efficient and effective operating environment in the federal government. To more accurately report on the number of pesticide products that are conditionally registered, OPP officials told us that the office has taken or planned to take the following actions:

- Beginning in the fall of 2010, representatives of the OPP divisions that deal with pesticide registrations began meeting with OPP management at least quarterly to, among other things, review proposed conditional registrations for pesticide products with new active ingredients to ensure that (1) any new conditional registrations granted for these products meet the circumstances outlined in FIFRA Section 3(c)(7)(C); (2) the additional data that would be requested as a part of the conditional registration are really needed; and (3) if the data are needed, EPA is still able to make the determination that the information available concerning the pesticide demonstrates that the FIFRA safety standard will be met, which requires that the use of the product during the time needed to generate the necessary data will not cause unreasonable adverse effects on the environment. According to OPP officials, since they started these quarterly reviews, the number of conditional registrations granted for new active ingredients generally has dropped. For example, since starting these reviews, they have been able to preclude cases of misclassification of new active ingredient registrations as "conditional" that had been occurring in the past. Specifically, they noted that, prior to 2010, in some cases, OPP staff had classified some of these registrations as conditional when the additional data being requested of the registrant could only be generated after the date of registration, such as data measuring the storage stability of a commercially manufactured version of the newly registered pesticide product. According to OPP officials, they do not regard such data requirements as being within the scope of FIFRA section 3(c)(7).

- In 2012, OPP began revising the registration categories in OPPIN to, among other things, more accurately reflect those circumstances under which conditional registrations may be granted under FIFRA. As of May 2013, OPP officials said that they had completed development of the categories and provided training to their regulatory staff on how to correctly assign the new categories to each type of registration. In July 2013, OPP officials said they had completed implementation of the new codes in OPPIN. In addition to the training, OPP officials noted the training materials will be available online for regulatory staff to consult for guidance on an ongoing basis.

- In fiscal year 2013, OPP began using a portion of the maintenance fees it collects to begin development of an electronic tracking system for conditional registrations. As discussed, OPP officials are not certain what the total cost of the system will be or when the system will be ready for implementation.

Table 1 summarizes the status, according to OPP officials, of key actions taken or planned by OPP to improve the reliability of conditional registration data.

Table 1: OPP Actions Taken or Planned to Improve the Reliability of Conditional Registration Data

Action	Planned completion date	Status	Potential barriers that may affect completion
Conduct quarterly OPP meetings to review the status of conditional registrations.	Ongoing	Began holding meetings in fall 2010.	None
Develop and implement new registration categories in OPPIN to more accurately reflect statutory basis for registration, including conditional registrations.	June 2013	Development of codes for these categories was completed in spring 2013. In July 2013, OPP officials indicated that they had completed the implementation of the new codes in OPPIN.	None
Train regulatory staff to use new codes.	Spring or summer 2013	Completed in spring 2013.	None
Design a new automated system that will include tools to improve the identification, tracking, reporting, and program management of conditional registrations.	2014 or beyond	In fiscal year 2013, began using a portion of the maintenance fees collected to start developing the system.	Complexity of system and size needed to manage the data. Availability of needed funding.

Source: EPA.

While OPP officials acknowledged the need to ensure that registrations are accurately classified to reflect their statutory basis and to develop an electronic data system for tracking the status of conditional registrations, they stated that EPA's past practices for managing conditional registrations have not created additional risks to the environment and have been in compliance with applicable laws. Specifically, an EPA attorney stated that the agency views products conditionally registered as identical or substantially similar to currently registered pesticides under section 3(c)(7)(A) and as new uses of currently registered pesticides under section 3(c)(7)(B) as meeting the same safety standards as products registered "unconditionally" under section 3(c)(5). Therefore, according to this official, these products do not pose unreasonable adverse effects on human health or the environment. Further, a Deputy Director of OPP said section 3(c)(7)(A) and section 3(c)(7)(B) registrations make up the bulk of conditionally registered pesticides. In addition, OPP officials stressed that the program actions that were mischaracterized as conditional registrations were nevertheless legitimate program actions. Specifically, these officials and OPP's website note that most of these actions were taken pursuant to the authority of FIFRA implementing regulations and should have been identified as such. Moreover, the EPA attorney stated that FIFRA does not require EPA to convert a registration from "conditional" to "unconditional" when all additional data requirements have been satisfied. So, according to this official, the fact that EPA has not done so in OPPIN in the past does not raise a legal issue. However, despite these assertions, EPA should still take steps to ensure that its data on the registration status of individual pesticide products are current and accurate.

Extent to Which EPA Ensures That Registrants Submit Additional Required Data and EPA Reviews These Data Is Unknown

The extent to which EPA ensures that registrants submit the additional data required when it grants conditional registrations or that it has reviewed these data is unknown. In particular, OPP does not have a reliable system, such as an automated data system, designed specifically to track key information related to conditional registrations, including whether registrants submitted additional data within required time frames and OPP reviewed these data. OPP officials acknowledged this lack of a comprehensive means to track the status of conditional registrations, and noted, as discussed, their intention to develop such a system. However, these officials, as well as OPP's website, note that the conditions for most of these registrations have likely been satisfied as a result of routine program operations that, in the OPP officials' view, constitute a quality assurance check. While these program operations may help to identify some situations where required data are missing, they fall short of what is needed because they are neither comprehensive nor do they ensure the timely submission of these data. This is a key reason that OPP officials are currently conducting a manual review of the files of the more than 16,000 active pesticide registrations OPP has issued, including conditional registrations, to identify any missing data, misclassified registrations, or other problems.

OPP's Lack of a Reliable System to Track Conditional Registrations Hinders Its Ability to Ensure that Data Are Submitted, Timely, and Reviewed

OPP lacks a reliable system specifically to track the status of conditional registrations to ensure that additional required data are submitted and timely, and that OPP reviews these data. As discussed, EPA currently "tracks" conditional registrations in OPPIN, an older data system that was not designed for this purpose and that does not have, among other things, the capability to flag situations in which required data have not been submitted by registrants or reviewed by OPP. Federal internal control standards require, in part, that information should be recorded and communicated to management and others within the entity who need it and in a form and within a time frame that enables them to carry out their internal control and other responsibilities.[28] Thus, for an entity to run and control its operations, it must obtain, maintain, and use relevant, reliable, and timely information for program oversight and decision making. Furthermore, the Office of Management and Budget (OMB) directs agency managers to take timely and effective action to correct internal control weaknesses.[29] As measured against this internal control standard, EPA's lack of a reliable and comprehensive means of routinely collecting and tracking information on conditional registrations, including the status of registrants' submission of required data and OPP's review of these data, constitutes an internal control weakness and leaves OPP without an important management tool. For example, when registrants miss due dates without applying for waivers or extensions, it is difficult for OPP without a reliable tracking system to identify these cases for priority follow-up and notify the registrants that their pesticide registrations could be cancelled.

In addition, without a reliable tracking system, OPP may miss conditional pesticides where, had the additional required data been submitted and reviewed, OPP might have altered the terms of a registration. OPP officials acknowledged there have been cases in which their consideration of these additional data led them to make minor changes to a registration, although they could not recall a case where these additional data prompted them to cancel a registration. These officials emphasized, and OPP documents state, that in issuing a conditional registration, even though OPP may ask the registrant for additional data, OPP has determined that the pesticide when used in accordance with labeling and common practices will not cause unreasonable adverse effects on the environment, and that OPP's registration decision takes into account the economic, social, and environmental costs and benefits of the use of that pesticide. Nevertheless, without the ability to systematically track conditional registrations, OPP is not well-positioned to produce summary data to enable it to easily identify situations for priority follow-up; enforce FIFRA and its implementing regulations; and report to Congress and others on program status. For example, without this tracking, it is more difficult to identify patterns of potential problems for management attention, such as registrants that are repeatedly late in

---

[28]GAO/AIMD-00-21.3.1.

[29]Office of Management and Budget, *Management's Responsibility for Internal Control*, OMB Circular No. A-123, Dec. 21, 2004.

providing additional required data for their conditional registrations, which could be the basis for canceling these registrations.

OPP's problems with data management have been well-documented over the years. GAO studies dating back to 1980, 1986, 1991 and 1992 noted problems with OPP data systems used to track the status of pesticide registrations.[30] For example, the 1986 study found that OPP did not have a data system for monitoring whether registrants were submitting the data required by conditional registrations and could only determine the status of data submissions by performing a time-consuming manual file search. At the time, we recommended that OPP take steps to review outstanding conditional registrations of new active ingredients and determine what progress is being made by registrants to submit the required data and take appropriate action. In response to our recommendation, OPP said it was developing a new automated system to track all outstanding data requirements. However, as discussed, OPP does not currently have such a system. The 1992 study noted that, after having spent $14 million over 3 years in data systems development, OPP could not easily assemble accurate, reliable, and complete information on pesticides subject to reregistration (now registration review). EPA Inspector General studies in 1994 and 2000 noted that OPP had not completed actions to improve information systems that contain inaccurate, incomplete, and duplicate data or that are not integrated.[31] In addition, a 2007 EPA contractor study found that many of these problems persist, especially with OPPIN.[32] Noting that OPPIN was launched in 2000,[33] this study found that this system had failed to meet the needs of OPP staff and that many of these staff had created "one-off" (off-line) tracking systems in order to get their jobs done, making comprehensive, reliable status updates, such as whether required data had been submitted and reviewed, very difficult to retrieve. The study also reported that OPPIN lacks the needed data fields and reporting functions for detailed tracking of the status of pesticide

---

[30]These reports are listed under "Related GAO Products" at the end of this report.

[31]EPA Office of Inspector General, *EPA's Pesticide Program*, Report no. E1EPE2-05-0015-4100205, Mar. 11, 1994; EPA Office of Inspector General, *Pesticides: Follow-up Report on EPA's Pesticide Program*, Report no. 00P00011, Mar. 27, 2000.

[32]EPA, *Evaluation of the U.S. EPA Pesticide Product Reregistration Process: Opportunities for Efficiency and Innovation*, March 2007, done by Abt Associates under EPA contract EP-W-04-023.

[33]According to EPA, although work on OPPIN began in 2000, the system was not operational until 2003.

registrations, and that multiple OPP staff had expressed dissatisfaction with OPPIN, stating that it is not user-friendly, data are not current or complete, and it lacks a "report card" function to easily check the status of pesticide registrations, including reregistration status. Although the contractor study noted that OPPIN was to be retired in September 2008, we found, as discussed, that OPP is still using OPPIN despite its many limitations.

Although Helpful in Identifying Missing Information, Routine Program Operations Fall Short of What Is Needed

OPP officials said, and the internal review states, that the conditions for most conditional registrations have likely been satisfied as a result of routine program operations that, in their view, constitute a quality assurance check. However, these operations fall short of what is needed for quality assurance because they are neither comprehensive nor do they ensure the timely submission of the additional data required as a condition of the registration. The program operations mentioned by OPP include the following:

- good faith submissions made by registrants to satisfy additional data requirements;
- record keeping and targeted follow-up done by pesticide product managers;
- state pesticide registration actions that may bring to light missing data required by the OPP's conditional registration of a pesticide;
- missing data identified as part of OPP's periodic reevaluation of registered pesticides; and
- registrant-initiated actions, such as label change amendments, that bring to light missing data associated with an earlier conditional registration.

The program operations OPP officials identified may help identify some situations where required data are missing, but they each have limitations and fall short of what is needed, as follows:

- *Registrant submissions:* While undoubtedly many registrants are conscientious about their timely submission of additional data required by their conditional registrations, OPP has found cases in the past where required data were not submitted or were submitted late. As discussed, once OPP issues a conditional registration, the registrant can move the associated pesticide product into the marketplace. In that sense, the registrant's commercialization of that product is not contingent on the registrant's submission of the additional required data. In addition, because OPPIN does not have the ability to systematically flag missing or late data, some registrants may be emboldened to delay or give less priority to developing and submitting these additional data.

- *Product manager actions:* The record keeping and targeted follow-up done by OPP product managers also have limitations. According to OPP officials, each of OPP's 20 product managers is responsible for tracking about 800 of the more than 16,000 active pesticide registrations maintained by OPP. While OPP officials acknowledged that each manager has a very broad span of control, there are other OPP regulatory staff who assist these managers. Moreover, of the approximately 800 registrations handled by each manager, conditional registrations constitute a subset, particularly for new active ingredients. However, we found that OPP had not provided written guidance to product managers on how to track the status of the pesticide registrations for which they are responsible. As a result, according to OPP officials, product managers use a variety of methods to track this information, including electronic spreadsheets or reminder notices, handwritten notes, and memory. Without OPP guidance on how product managers should maintain their pesticide registration files, in the case of the retirement or resignation of an experienced manager—or even the extended absence of a manager due to illness—other managers asked to replace or fill in for this manager may not be familiar with how he or she maintained files or data, or the extent to which this official relied on memory versus written records. Furthermore, requiring all product managers to track the status of registrations in a consistent, electronic format would help OPP meet the goals of an August 2012 OMB directive that, among other things, directs executive agencies to the fullest extent possible to eliminate paper and use electronic record keeping to ensure transparency, efficiency, and accountability. The directive is applicable to all executive agencies and all records.[34]

- *State registration:* While state pesticides registration activities may help to bring to light missing data associated with conditional registrations issued by OPP, the extent to which this happens is unknown and should not be relied upon as a quality assurance check. After OPP registers a pesticide, states also can register that pesticide

---

[34]OMB, Managing Government Records Directive, M-12-18, Aug. 24, 2012.

GAO-13-145 Conditional Pesticide Registration

under specific state pesticide registration laws. A state may be more stringent in registering a pesticide for use in that state, but its registration requirements generally may not be less stringent than the federal requirements. In addition, states generally have primary responsibility (known as "primacy") for enforcement of the proper use of pesticides within their borders.

- *Periodic review of registered pesticides:* As discussed, FIFRA requires that EPA periodically reevaluate registered pesticides to ensure that each registration continues to satisfy regulatory standards. EPA originally did this reevaluation under its reregistration program, applicable to pesticides registered prior to November 1984. More recently, this reevaluation is being done under the agency's registration review program. According to OPP officials, this periodic review of previously registered pesticides provides an opportunity to identify missing data required by a conditional registration. For example, these officials said any missing data related to section 3(c)(7)(A) (identical or similar) or (B) (new uses) can be identified through registration review. They explained that registrations under these sections do not impose new data requirements. Instead, these registrations are issued when there is an outstanding DCI, or planned DCI, for an identical or similar currently registered pesticide. Thus, according to OPP officials, because registrations under these sections are linked to DCIs, and OPP's Pesticide Registration Information System (PRISM) is used to track DCIs,[35] they are confident in their ability to ensure the timely submission of required data. They noted that PRISM is a newer and more robust data system than OPPIN. They also noted that (1) most conditional registrations are made under sections 3(c)(7)(A) or (B), (2) the associated DCIs place a legal obligation on the registrant to provide the requested data, and (3) OPP may suspend a registration for failure to respond to a DCI. However, we note that PRISM has apparent limitations as well. For example, OPP officials said that PRISM is not designed, per se, to track conditional registrations and therefore cannot be used to identify the conditional registrations, if any, associated with a particular DCI. In addition, they said while this system is useful for tracking the status of DCIs on a case-by-case basis, PRISM lacks the capability to produce summary reports for management attention that could

---

[35]PRISM is an OPP data system that is intended to provide a centralized source of information on all registered pesticide products, including chemical composition, toxicity, name and address of registrant, brand names, registration actions, and related data.

GAO-13-145 Conditional Pesticide Registration

indicate, for example, the extent to which registrants are meeting the requirement to provide an initial response to a DCI within 90 days.[36]

Furthermore, as acknowledged by OPP officials, registration review is not helpful in tracking the status of conditional registrations made for new active ingredients under FIFRA section 3(c)(7)(C). For these registrations, there is no relationship to an identical or similar, currently registered pesticide. As a result, the potential exists that a conditionally registered pesticide under this section would continue to be sold and used in the United States for a number of years before OPP discovered that the additional data required had not been submitted and were late. In reviewing OPP documents related to the conditional registration of new active ingredients done in the early 2000s, we noted such cases. In each case, when the associated pesticide product came up for registration review, OPP determined that some of the required data related to the original conditional registration had not been submitted and were late or, if submitted, had not been reviewed by OPP. For example, in the case of a pesticide product containing the active ingredient Foramsulfuron, conditionally registered in November 2002, two required studies on the effects of this pesticide on terrestrial and aquatic plants that were due in December 2004 had not been submitted 10 years after the conditional registration was issued, as determined by OPP's registration review of this pesticide in 2012.[37] In another case, involving a pesticide product containing the active ingredient Acetamiprid, conditionally registered in March 2002, OPP discovered during its registration review of this pesticide in 2012, about 10 years later, that it had received, but not reviewed, a study related to the effects of this pesticide on honeybees. OPP documents indicate the registrant submitted this study in 2001, even before OPP granted the conditional registration. Acetamiprid belongs to a class of pesticides called neonicotinoids that some beekeepers, environmental groups, and others suspect of having adverse effects on honeybees.

---

[36]In July 2013, in its technical comments on a draft of this report, EPA stated that PRISM is now capable of producing summary reports for management. However, the agency neither explained what these reports are nor did it provide examples.

[37]In July 2013, in its technical comments on a draft of this report, EPA said that after contacting the registrant and determining that the registrant did not intend to fulfill the requirements of its conditional registration for this product, the agency cancelled the registration in February 2013 (78 FR 8513, Feb. 6, 2013). The registrations of other pesticide products containing Foramsulfuron were not affected by this cancellation.

- *Registrant-initiated actions:* According to OPP officials, if a registrant applies to amend a registration, such as to make a label change, this action triggers an OPP review of the data supporting the pesticide registration and provides an opportunity to identify missing data associated with a conditional registration. If it is determined that data are missing, the agency may issue a DCI requiring the registrant to provide the data by a specific date. However, this mechanism to identify missing data is ad hoc and only applies to cases in which a registrant seeks to amend its registration.

In addition, OPP officials pointed to an analysis they performed as part of OPP's 2011 internal review that showed registrants usually meet the additional data requirements associated with their conditional registrations on a timely basis. Specifically, OPP examined 544 conditional registrations that it granted (1) for new uses or new active ingredients under FIFRA sections (3(c)(7)(B) or (C), respectively, and (2) from March 2004 to September 2010. According to OPP officials and the office's website, these conditional registrations were selected because, as relatively recent registrations, they were the most likely candidates to be missing additional required data. In contrast, according to OPP officials, older conditional registrations were less likely to be missing data because of the application of the cited routine program operations.

To do this analysis, OPP officials said they first identified all additional data requirements and associated due dates for these conditional registrations, and then manually reviewed the files for these pesticides to determine if the required data were submitted and due dates met. When finished, OPP concluded that registrants had completed 96 percent of "all actions intended" for these 544 conditional registrations in a timely manner. OPP posted this information on its website. However, in reviewing the information on the website, as well as supporting documents provided by OPP, we were unable to verify these calculations, in part because OPP was unable to locate some of the supporting documentation. In addition, some of the documentation provided did not always make clear whether the submitted data had been timely or reviewed by OPP. Furthermore, we found that some of the statements on the website were confusing; used technical terms such as "registration," "action," and "decision" without defining the terms; and contained other discrepancies. Some of these problems have been cited by legal and environmental groups who found this information confusing as well. Although OPP officials generally agreed that revisions were needed to the discussion on the website for clarity, OPP had no specific plan or time frame for doing so. Regardless of any clarifications needed to the website, an OPP Deputy Director expressed confidence in the results of this analysis. As of July 2013, the discussion of this analysis on the website had not been clarified.

OPP Is Manually Reviewing All of the More than 16,000 Pesticide Registrations to Identify Problems Such as Missing Data

In May 2012, OPP staff began manually reviewing the files for the more than 16,000 pesticide registrations granted by EPA. The purposes of this review include identifying all outstanding data requirements, as well as cases where the registration action, such as a label change amendment, was mischaracterized as a "conditional registration." According to OPP officials, all prior registrations are being reviewed, not just those classified as conditional, because pesticide registrations may have long histories, and even though a registration may have been classified initially as unconditional, OPP may have imposed additional data requirements at a later time.

According to OPP officials, reviewing each pesticide registration file is time-consuming and, depending on the pesticide, may take from a few hours to a few days to complete. This generally includes OPP regulatory staff reviewing voluminous paper files associated with many of these pesticide registrations. According to these officials, once this review process is completed, OPP will have a "clean" set of data that will, among other things, identify (1) any missing data, (2) missed deadlines for registrants submitting these data, and (3) cases where the registration action was mischaracterized, including the misuse of "conditional registration." These officials said the review results are being recorded in an electronic spreadsheet, known as the "master file," for future use. For example, when a pesticide comes up for registration review, OPP officials said that staff will refer to the master file to identify any missing data that should be included in the DCI resulting from that review.

Although OPP's review of prior pesticide registrations remains a work in progress, OPP provided an excerpt from its electronic spreadsheet showing the results for three pesticides that we asked about because other agency documents we reviewed suggested possible registration issues. For these pesticides, the spreadsheet indicated that most, but not all, of the required data had been submitted by registrants; some of these data were submitted from 2 to 12 months after the related due dates and, for one of these pesticides, no due date was specified in the registration notice, making it impossible to determine if the data were submitted on-time. In this last case, OPP officials stated that the lack of due dates in the registration notice was an unintentional oversight. Since OPP has not finished its review of all prior registrations, it has not yet developed summary statistics on the frequency with which these types of problems were found. OPP officials said they plan to complete their manual review of prior registrations by the fall of 2013, but its completion by then will depend on the amount of time OPP staff can devote to this review relative to their other responsibilities. In addition, according to agency officials, by the end of calendar year 2013, they plan to make public information from the review about the number of active ingredients approved under FIFRA section 3(c)(7)(C) for which data are overdue, and those for which data were submitted late.

While OPP's manual review of existing registrations may result in a clean data set and identify some missing data and other problems not discovered as a result of what OPP calls routine program operations, it is an interim measure. Among other things, OPP officials said their office needs a comprehensive automated data system for tracking conditional registrations. As noted by one OPP division director, "no one wants to have to track this information by hand" in the future. In addition, according to these officials, OPP does not plan to update the master file to include new pesticide registrations or other registration changes that occur in the future. They noted that the master file is retrospective, and it provides a snapshot in time. Instead, OPP officials said that new pesticide registrations and other registration changes will be entered into OPPIN using the new codes that OPPIN plans to introduce in June 2013. In July 2013, EPA advised us that the codes have been entered in OPPIN. According to these officials, the introduction of these new codes, in conjunction with staff training on how to use them, should preclude some of the misclassification problems experienced in the past until a new comprehensive data system is available to replace OPPIN.

Stakeholders Generally Said EPA Needs to Improve Its Conditional Registration Process and Had Mixed Views on the Value of These Registrations

The 24 stakeholders that responded to our questionnaire—including representatives of consumer (3), environmental (6), industry (5), legal (3), producer (1), science (1), and state government groups (5)—generally indicated that EPA needs to improve its conditional registration process and, in some cases, they offered suggestions for improving this process.[38] The issues that stakeholders raised included concerns about the timely submission and review of required data and the misuse of the conditional registration designation. In addition, stakeholders' views varied regarding the potential benefits and problems associated with the conditional registration of pesticides.

Respondents Generally Reported That EPA Needs to Improve Its Conditional Registration Process

In responding to our questionnaire, respondents in the consumer, environmental, industry, legal, science, and state government stakeholder groups generally reported concerns with submission or review of required data as follows:

- Of the 19 respondents in the consumer, environmental, legal, producer, science, and state government groups, 17 reported concerns related to registrants not submitting additional required data on time, including concerns about pesticides that remain in the marketplace when their environmental and health impacts have not been fully evaluated.[39] In addition, 3 of the 8 respondents from consumer groups and state government were generally concerned that, when registrants are allowed to miss due dates without any follow-up from EPA, there is little incentive for the registrants to submit the additional data and take the data requirements seriously. Further, 4 of the 17 respondents from consumer, environmental, legal, and state government groups reported that EPA should cancel registrations for those registrants who do not submit required data on time.

---

[38]Not every stakeholder responded to every question. The questions were open-ended and thus issues raised by stakeholders had to be "volunteered." We did not ask each stakeholder to agree or disagree with particular issues.

[39]OPP officials noted that they share these concerns, but they stated that the results of OPP's internal review of conditional registrations convinced them that these concerns have no basis.

- Of the 19 respondents from environmental, industry, legal, and state government groups, 8 reported concerns about EPA's record keeping related to conditional registrations, including the agency's ability to ensure the receipt and review of required data. Specifically, one industry stakeholder stated that EPA does not effectively track the receipt and review of required data and said, in particular, EPA does not always acknowledge receipt of required information and does not always notify recipients whether the data submitted satisfied the condition.[40] However, 4 of the 5 respondents from industry stated the public faced little risk when required data are not submitted or reviewed, pointing out that before EPA conditionally registers a pesticide, the agency must determine that the pesticide meets FIFRA registration standards.

Stakeholders representing environmental, industry, and state government groups generally reported concern with EPA issuing conditional registrations for circumstances that were outside of the permissible situations stated in FIFRA. Examples are as follows:

- Of the 16 respondents representing these groups, 10 reported concern that EPA was overusing conditional registrations. Three of the 5 environmental stakeholders that had these concerns generally stated that conditional registrations were originally intended to be used in limited circumstances where a public need was established—such as the need to quickly approve the use of a pesticide to prevent significant crop damage and economic loss—and that EPA's current practices for issuing conditional registrations are not in keeping with this original intent.[41]

- Of the 5 respondents from industry, 3 stated that there are cases when EPA grants a conditional registration for a pesticide that should have qualified for an unconditional registration. These stakeholders reported that, in some of these cases, EPA had granted a conditional

---

[40]EPA officials noted that there is no legal requirement for EPA to acknowledge receipt of required information or notify registrants whether the data submitted satisfy the condition imposed.

[41]EPA officials noted that the public interest finding only applies to FIFRA section 3(c)(7)(C) related to conditional registration of pesticide products with new active ingredients, and not to sections 3(c)(7)(A) or (B) related to conditional registration of products that are identical or substantially similar to products already registered or new uses of products already registered, respectively.

registration for reasons that were outside of those permissible circumstances outlined in FIFRA, such as the need for labeling changes and potential data requirements that could be imposed in the future as a result of the registration review process. Of these three industry stakeholders, two were aware of EPA's recent efforts to ensure that conditional registrations are granted only in appropriate circumstances, as described on the agency's website, and these stakeholders were supportive of these efforts.

In keeping with these concerns, respondents from environmental, industry, producer, and state government groups generally offered suggestions for improving EPA's conditional registration process. Following are examples:

- Of the 16 respondents representing environmental, industry, and state government groups, 7 generally stated that EPA needs a better system for tracking the status of conditional registrations, including its review of required data.

- Of the 10 respondents representing industry and state government groups, 6 stated that it would be helpful if EPA developed a way to share information about conditional registrations with external stakeholders. For example, a respondent from a state government group suggested that EPA create a notification and tracking system for states that specifically lists the status of conditional registrations and any pending data requirements. The stakeholder stated that this system would facilitate the exchange of information between EPA and the states. Also, a respondent representing an industry group stated that EPA should develop a system similar to one used by California's Department of Pesticide Regulation; the respondent stated that this system allows registrants to access information on the status of their pesticide registration applications pending before that state and about their conditionally registered products.

- Of the 5 industry respondents, 2 suggested that EPA address concerns about overuse of conditional registrations by taking steps to ensure that these registrations only are used according to the explicit criteria set forth in FIFRA section 3(c)(7).

Some Respondents Stated That Conditional Registrations Offer Benefits, and Others Stated That They Pose Serious Risks

Of the 17 respondents representing consumer, industry, legal, producer, and state government groups, 14 stated that there were significant benefits in conditionally registering pesticides. They generally noted that the conditional registration process is an important and effective mechanism that gives EPA the flexibility to allow pesticides to move to the market more quickly, and that quicker movement to the market, in turn, provides users and growers with faster access to the pesticides they need. For example, one respondent commented that conditional registrations are especially valuable in situations where users have a much more limited choice of pesticides that meet their needs, such as growers of specialty crops.[42] Seven of these 14 respondents also generally stated that conditional registrations promote innovation by bringing new technologies and products to the marketplace faster.

In contrast, 13 of the 18 respondents representing consumer, environmental, legal, science, and state government groups stated that there were numerous negative impacts caused by conditionally registering pesticides. For example, all 13 of the respondents concerned with negative impacts reported that conditionally registering pesticides can delay EPA's ability to mitigate public health and environmental impacts caused by pesticides. These respondents generally stated that EPA is not conducting a full, rigorous review of conditionally registered pesticides and therefore is allowing these pesticides into the marketplace without complete data, such as toxicity tests and studies that demonstrate the pesticides' impact on the environment. Eight of these 13 respondents who expressed concern with conditionally registering a new use of a pesticide generally noted that, without a full, rigorous review, EPA may miss problems caused by the new use that may not have occurred with the original use.[43] Four of the 13 respondents also stated that, especially in the cases that involve pesticides with new active ingredients, a conditional registration should only be granted if a critical need for the pesticide can be demonstrated. Six of the 13 respondents stated that the risks posed by conditionally registering new active ingredients were so great that EPA should discontinue this type of conditional registration. In

[42]Specialty crops include fruits and vegetables, tree nuts, dried fruits, and nursery crops (e.g., flowers).

[43]EPA officials stated that EPA must have all of the data pertaining to a new use of a pesticide before approving the use. Thus, according to these officials, EPA fully evaluates the human health and environmental impacts of adding the new use.

elaborating on their concerns, 12 of the 18 respondents from consumer, environmental, legal, science, and state government groups cited examples of conditionally registered pesticides that, in their opinion, should not have been conditionally registered. The three pesticide products mentioned most frequently by these respondents were the following:

Clothianidin

Background: According to EPA documents, in 2003, EPA conditionally registered the insecticide Clothianidin, which the agency had identified as an alternative to older, more toxic insecticides. As one of the conditions of the registration, EPA required the manufacturer, Bayer CropScience, to submit a study evaluating the effects on honeybees of prolonged exposure to Clothianidin. In 2007, the agency reviewed this study and determined that it satisfied EPA's field study guidelines. However, in 2010 and again in 2012, numerous entities, including consumer and environmental groups, petitioned EPA to discontinue use of Clothianidin, charging, among other things, that it posed an imminent hazard to honeybees. In 2010, EPA decided to reevaluate the study and ultimately determined that there were some deficiencies in the study but that the registered uses of Clothianidin met the FIFRA standard for registration. According to Bayer CropScience, the use of Clothianidin was necessary to prevent crop damage from pesticide-resistant pests and the dying of honeybees in 2008, which environmental groups claimed was caused by Clothianidin, was actually a result of a variety of factors, including incorrect application of the pesticide.

Stakeholder comments: Half (9 of 18) of the respondents representing consumer, environmental, legal, science, and state government groups raised concerns about the insecticide Clothianidin. For example, of the 9 respondents who raised concerns, 6 generally reported that EPA should not have conditionally registered this pesticide in 2003 without all the data needed to establish that the pesticide would not significantly increase unreasonable adverse effects to pollinators, including honeybees. Two of these 6 respondents reported that the failure to do so has allowed the widespread use of a pesticide that, in their view, has caused the death of honeybee colonies and irreparably damaged the environment and livelihoods of beekeepers. Four of the 6 respondents said that it is irresponsible for EPA to refuse to discontinue the registration of this product when the agency eventually determined that the pollinator study submitted by the company was inadequate.[44]

Imprelis

Background: According to EPA documents, in August 2010, EPA conditionally registered the active ingredient of the pesticide Imprelis. This pesticide, manufactured by DuPont, was a low-toxicity herbicide used to control weeds, vines, and grasses on nonfood use sites, such as weeds around an office building. EPA stated that the studies originally submitted for Imprelis were adequate to make a finding for the registration but also concluded that two additional studies (on toxicity and reproduction) were required to confirm the conclusions from existing data. However, in the summer of 2011, EPA received reports from several states that this pesticide may have caused injury to certain species of evergreen trees, particularly Norway spruce and white pine. In a June 2011 letter, DuPont cautioned professional applicators not to use Imperils near certain species of trees, including Norway spruce and white pine. On August 4, 2011, DuPont voluntarily suspended sales of Imprelis and, on August 11, 2011, EPA issued a stop-sale order directing DuPont to immediately halt the sale, use, or distribution of Imprelis. According to EPA, it issued this stop-sale order because it had reason to believe the product was misbranded and the agency had obtained new information, not available during the registration process, that showed Imprelis was toxic to certain trees. Currently, EPA is evaluating the tree damage to determine what caused the injuries. DuPont has since started a return and refund program for Imprelis users.

Stakeholder comments: Of the 7 respondents representing environmental and science groups, 4 raised concerns about the pesticide Imprelis. According to 3 of these 4 stakeholders, EPA did not properly consider the "unreasonable effects on the environment" of this pesticide, specifically effects on organisms that this pesticide was not intended kill, including trees. One stakeholder reported that the experience with this pesticide illustrates what can happen when EPA allows a pesticide product to proceed to the marketplace without complete information and, in this

[44]As of January 2013, EPA officials noted that the agency is considering a request for suspension of this product. EPA denied a previous request to suspend this product. According to these officials, the current suspension request is based on a dispute related to the science underlying the registration, not the fact that the registration is conditional per se. EPA officials also noted that because EPA is involved in active litigation on Clothianidin, they are unable to respond to these stakeholder comments.

stakeholder's opinion, confirms that the conditional registration process actually allows EPA to bypass statutory safeguards and rush pesticides with unknown and unevaluated risks to market.[45]

Nanosilver

Background: According to EPA documents, in December 2011, EPA issued a conditional registration for a pesticide product containing nanosilver as a new active ingredient. As we reported in May 2010, nanosilver is one of a number of nanomaterials, which are materials that occur at the scale of nanometers—the equivalent of one-billionth of a meter, increasingly being used in commercial and industrial products.[46] The antimicrobial pesticide product, HeiQ AGS-20, is a silver-based nanomaterial for use as a preservative for textiles. As a condition of registration, EPA is requiring the registrant, HeiQ Materials AG, to submit a number of studies to confirm the agency's assessment that the product will not cause unreasonable adverse effects on the environment. These studies include toxicity studies for occupational, residential, and environmental exposure scenarios.[47] The data must be submitted within 4 years (i.e., by December 2015) to avoid cancellation of the conditional registration. The registrant agreed with the agency's decision to grant a conditional registration. The registrant stated that this registration was

---

[45]EPA officials noted that the additional data it required for the conditional registration of Imprelis were related to human health, specifically dietary/food exposure. According to these officials, EPA received required studies from the company related to nontarget plants. EPA reviewed these studies, found no concerns, and the product was conditionally approved. However, after the product was marketed, it became apparent that it was killing trees. According to EPA officials, based on the studies the company submitted, there was no reason to suspect that the product would impact trees. However, a study specifically for effects on trees was neither required by EPA nor submitted by the company. EPA officials stated that the tree deaths were very unfortunate and made the product unacceptable and that if EPA had known about the impacts on trees at the time the product was being considered for registration, the agency might not have registered the product at all. EPA officials stated that this was not a case where the agency failed to anticipate risks, rather, it was a risk that the standard data requirements did not capture and a risk that only came to light after the product was registered and marketed.

[46]GAO, *Nanotechnology: Nanomaterials Are Widely Used in Commerce, but EPA Faces Challenges in Regulating Risk,* GAO-10-549 (Washington, D.C.: May 25, 2010).

[47]EPA has previously addressed toxicity concerns regarding nanosilver. In 2010, EPA issued its *State of the Science Literature Review: Everything Nanosilver and More* in which EPA reported that there is clear evidence that nanosilver is toxic to aquatic and terrestrial organisms and may be detrimental to human health. In this report, EPA noted that several studies have shown that nanosilver can be released into the wastewater stream during washing, such as from socks containing nanosilver. The nanosilver released may disrupt the helpful bacteria used in wastewater treatment processes or be released into the environment.

appropriate because (1) the company had insufficient time to generate certain required data, (2) use of the pesticide is in the public interest, and (3) use of the pesticide during the period needed to generate and review the required data will not cause unreasonable adverse effects. The registration of this product is being challenged in a lawsuit by the Natural Resources Defense Council.[48]

Stakeholder comments: Eight of the 18 respondents representing consumer, environmental, legal, science, and state government groups raised concerns about the conditional registration of the nanosilver product HeiQ AGS-20. Among other things, these respondents stated that there was a significant lack of data needed to fully evaluate the safety of this product, including a lack of data on potential human health effects. One stakeholder pointed out that silver is highly toxic to both humans and the environment and, when used at the nanoscale level, the science is still developing on how such nanoparticles behave. Another stakeholder said this conditional registration is particularly troubling because EPA's Office of the Inspector General recently concluded that the EPA lacks an effective program to collect information and monitor the possible health risks posed by nanomaterials,[49] and because the National Research Council similarly found that the federal government needs an improved plan and additional funding to assess the environmental and health risks posed by nanomaterials.[50]

Conclusions

OPP faces a formidable task in managing the registrations of more than 16,000 pesticide products. This includes periodically reconsidering whether older registrations continue to meet the regulatory standard and

---

[48]EPA officials said that the basis of the Natural Resources Defense Council lawsuit is not a challenge of EPA's use of conditional registrations under FIFRA section 3(c)(7) or whether EPA met the standards for granting a conditional registration under this statute. Rather, according to these officials, the lawsuit questions an aspect of the risk assessment methodology that EPA used in this case to make the determination of no unreasonable adverse effects.

[49]EPA Office of the Inspector General, *EPA Needs to Manage Nanomaterial Risks More Effectively,* Report no. 12-P-0162, Dec. 29, 2011. OPP officials noted that the Office of the Inspector General advised EPA to develop a better internal process for sharing data across program offices. According to these officials, EPA has implemented this recommendation, and an Inspector General official concurred.

[50]National Research Council of the National Academies, *A Research Strategy for Environmental, Health, and Safety Aspects of Engineered Nanomaterials,* the National Academies Press (Washington, D.C.: 2012).

reviewing applications submitted each year for new or amended registrations. The pesticide products that the agency registers play a critical role in food production by helping to minimize crop losses due to pests and weeds. In addition, pesticide products have helped improve public health by controlling disease-carrying pests, such as insects and rodents. At the same time, consumers rely on OPP to ensure that registered pesticide products do not cause unreasonable adverse effects on the environment or human health when used according to the label instructions approved by the agency.

OPP faces challenges in tracking key information specifically related to conditional registrations, and, as a result, is unable to produce accurate information on the current number of these registrations. OPP's lack of a reliable and comprehensive means of routinely collecting and tracking information on conditional registrations, including the status of registrants' submission of required data and OPP's review of these data, leaves it without an important management tool. Because OPP is not systematically tracking whether registrants of conditionally registered pesticides submitted additional required data, and whether OPP reviewed these data, it may not be able to identify situations in which the additional data would suggest the need to alter a registration. Furthermore, without the ability to systematically track conditional registrations, OPP is not well-positioned to produce summary data to enable it to easily identify situations for priority follow-up; enforce FIFRA and its implementing regulations; and report to Congress and others on program status.

Furthermore, OPP's use of conditional registrations for actions other than those that meet the criteria outlined in FIFRA Section 3(c)(7) has created confusion for its staff, and may leave OPP vulnerable to charges by environmental, industry, and other stakeholders who assert that it inappropriately grants conditional registrations. According to OPP officials and documents, weaknesses in guidance and training, management oversight, and data management contributed to the misclassification of other pesticide-related activities as conditional registrations. OPP has raised the visibility of these issues by holding meetings at least quarterly with representatives of the OPP divisions that issue pesticide registrations to discuss any conditional registrations being considered for new active ingredients to ensure they meet the statutory criteria outlined in FIFRA Section 3(c)(7) and that the additional information requested is indeed needed to unconditionally register the pesticide. In addition, OPP has taken or plans to take other actions to ensure that staff appropriately grant conditional registrations and registrants submit required data; however, these are short-term solutions that do not fully address the problems identified. As OPP officials and stakeholders recognize, OPP needs a comprehensive automated data system to track conditional registrations from the time the conditional registration is granted until additional data requested is received and reviewed. However, OPP previously stated over 25 years ago that it planned to develop an automated system for tracking conditional registrations of new active ingredients, but it did not follow through with this plan. OPP has secured funding through FIFRA amendments to begin the development of such a system, but much work remains to be done and will depend on a further commitment of needed resources.

Moreover, OPP lacks written guidance or a consistent methodology for how product managers are to maintain their pesticide registration files. Allowing product managers to use disparate methods to collect and keep information on the pesticides they are responsible for makes it more difficult to develop summary information about the status of pesticide registrations overall, which could be useful information for managing the pesticide registration program. Also, as the extensive amount of time and effort needed in OPP's ongoing review of all registered pesticides demonstrates, product managers' current methods are not sufficient to efficiently track this information. It will take time and money to develop an automated system for tracking the progress of conditionally registered pesticides but, in the interim, OPP is further hampered in its efforts to be informed about the status of conditional registrations because product managers do not use a consistent system for tracking their status, including when data are submitted by registrants and reviewed by OPP. Furthermore, OPP's reliance on the institutional knowledge of its product managers and the records they keep is problematic for other reasons, including the loss of knowledge and experience of these employees as they retire or are replaced by new employees.

Finally, OPP has also not clearly and concisely communicated the results of its analyses of conditional registrations on its website. It is important for agencies to ensure that information placed on their websites is accurate and free of discrepancies. OPP officials have acknowledged the need to correct the agency's website on conditional registrations and remove any confusing or inaccurate statements.

Recommendations for Executive Action

To improve EPA's management of the conditional registration process, we recommend that the Administrator of EPA direct the Director of the Office of Pesticide Programs to take the following three actions:

- Complete plans to automate data related to conditional registrations to more readily track the status of these registrations and related registrant and agency actions and identify potential problems requiring management attention,

- Pending development of an automated data system for tracking the status of conditional registrations, develop guidance to ensure that product managers use a uniform methodology to track and document this information, including when data are submitted by registrants and reviewed by EPA, in the files maintained by each pesticide product manager.

- Review and correct, as appropriate, OPP's website on conditional registrations to ensure that the information presented is clear, concise, and accurate, including defining technical terms.

Agency Comments and Our Evaluation

We provided a draft of this report to EPA for review and comment. In written comments, which are included in appendix II, EPA agreed with the report's recommendations. Regarding the first recommendation, EPA said that its implementation plan to automate data related to conditional registrations includes (1) development of new codes for identifying conditional registration decisions in OPPIN; (2) training its staff on use of the new categories represented by these new codes, and making the training available online for guidance; and (3) changes to its databases to allow staff to check more easily whether there are any outstanding requests for data on any pesticide active ingredients. EPA also said it plans to develop a more comprehensive system for tracking conditional registrations; however, the agency's ability to do so depends on the availability of funding and the complexity of incorporating changes in the databases. Regarding the second recommendation, EPA said it is developing a standard operating procedure for staff to follow when entering data into the computerized tracking system about the statutory basis for registration decisions. According to EPA, this procedure, together with the new training for staff, should ensure that conditional registration decisions are properly identified in the OPPIN database going forward. The agency said it expects to complete the procedure by the end of calendar year 2013. EPA added that the status of products previously approved under conditional registration authority is also being reviewed and updated, as necessary. For the third recommendation, EPA said by the end of 2013 it will revise its website on conditional registration to both clarify and update the information presented. In addition, EPA indicated the website will include an outline of ongoing agency work to strengthen its conditional pesticide registration program. EPA also provided technical comments, which we incorporated as appropriate.

As agreed with your office, unless you publicly announce the contents of this report earlier, we will plan no further distribution until 30 days from the report date. At that time, we will send copies of this report to the Administrator of EPA, the appropriate congressional committees, and other interested parties. In addition, the report will be available at no charge on the GAO website at http://www.gao.gov.

If you or your staff members have any questions about this report, please contact me at (202) 512-3841 or gomezj@gao.gov. Contact points for our Offices of Congressional Relations and Public Affairs may be found on the last page of this report. GAO staff who made key contributions to this report are listed in appendix III.

Sincerely yours,

Alfredo Gómez

J. Alfredo Gómez
Director, Natural Resources and Environment

Appendix I: Objectives, Scope and Methodology

Our objectives were to examine the (1) number of conditional pesticide registrations the Environmental Protection Agency (EPA) has granted and the basis for granting these registrations; (2) extent to which EPA ensures that registrants submit the additional data EPA required as part of conditional registrations and reviews these data; and (3) views of relevant stakeholders on EPA's use of conditional registrations, including ways, if any, to improve the conditional registration process. To address these objectives, we reviewed relevant federal statutes and regulations,[1] EPA program and guidance documents,[2] federal internal control standards,[3] and previous GAO and EPA Inspector General reports.[4] We also reviewed EPA's fiscal year 2011–2015 strategic plan; EPA's fiscal year 2011 and 2012 annual performance plans; EPA's budget justification documents for fiscal years 2012 and 2013; Office of Pesticide Programs' (OPP) pesticide registration work plans for fiscal years 2001 through 2012; OPP notices of pesticide registration for conditionally registered pesticides; and Federal Register notices related to OPP's registration decisions. In addition, we interviewed OPP officials and reviewed documentation they provided to obtain further information and clarification

---

[1]These statutes and regulations include *Federal Insecticide, Fungicide, and Rodenticide Act,* Act of June 25, 1947, ch. 125, 61 Stat. 163 (codified as amended at 7 U.S.C. §§ 136-136y); *Federal Food, Drug, and Cosmetic Act,* 21 U.S.C. §§ 301-399f; *Food Quality Protection Act of 1996,* Pub. L. No. 104-170 110 Stat. 1489; *Pesticide Registration Improvement Act of 2003,* Pub. L. No. 108-199 Div. G. Tit. V. § 501. 118 Stat. 419 (2004); and relevant parts from title 20 of *the Code of Federal Regulations.*

[2]These program and guidance documents included EPA, *Conditional Registrations – Summary and Analysis,* Office of Pesticide Program Internal Review, Spring 2011; *Pesticide Programs: Conditional Registration of New Pesticides,* F.R. Vol. 51, No. 43, p.p. 7628-7634; and EPA Biological and Economic Analysis Division (BEAD), *Guidance for BEAD Review: Public Interest Findings for Conditional Registration.*

[3]GAO, *Internal Control Management and Evaluation Tool,* GAO-01-1008G (Washington, D.C.: August 2001); GAO/AIMD-00-21.3.1; Office of Management and Budget, *Management's Responsibility for Internal Control,* OMB Circular No. A-123, Dec. 21, 2004; Office of Management and Budget, *Managing Government Records Directive,* M-12-18, Aug. 24, 2012.

[4]Previous GAO reports reviewed are listed in "Related GAO Products" at the end of this report. Previous EPA Inspector General reports include: EPA Office of Inspector General, *EPA Needs to Manage Nanomaterial Risks More Effectively,* Report no. 12-P-0162, Dec. 29, 2011; EPA Office of Inspector General, *EPA Needs to Comply with the Federal Insecticide, Fungicide, and Rodenticide Act and Improve Its Oversight of Exported Never-Registered Pesticides,* Report no. 10-P-0026, Nov. 10, 2009; EPA Office of Inspector General, *Office of Inspector General Semiannual Report to the Congress,* Report no. EPA-350-K-00-002, November 2000; EPA Office of Inspector General, *EPA's Pesticide Program,* Report no. E1EPE2-05-0015-4100205, Mar. 11, 1994.

on EPA's conditional registration process, including any planned responses to internal review or external stakeholder concerns. Furthermore, we reviewed recent literature related to pesticide registration, including information and documents found on the websites of a variety of consumer, environmental, industry, legal, producer, science, and state government organizations.

To examine the number of conditional pesticide registrations EPA has granted and the basis for them, we requested that OPP provide us with summary data on (1) the number of pesticide registrations currently in conditional status and how long they have been in this status; (2) the total number of current pesticide registrations (conditional and unconditional); and (3) for fiscal years 1997 through 2011, the number of conditional registrations granted for each year and the basis on which these were granted. We asked for information for 1997 through 2011 because reviewing registrations from this period could address the concerns that environmental and other groups raised that some pesticides may have been in conditional status for many years and also take into account key changes made to the pesticide registration and tolerance setting processes that occurred after 1996.[5] We intended to assess the reliability of the data that we requested from EPA and conduct electronic testing on data fields necessary for our analysis; however, after interviewing OPP officials and reviewing past GAO, Inspector General, and EPA contractor studies examining OPP's data management, especially its use of the Office of Pesticide Programs Information Network (OPPIN), we concluded that EPA could not provide us with sufficiently reliable data for obtaining summary level information on conditional pesticide registrations. In the absence of these data, we discussed with OPP officials the capabilities and limitations of OPPIN and any potential work-arounds they employ or are planning for. In addition, we reviewed and discussed with these officials a recent analysis of OPPIN data that OPP conducted to determine how many of the conditional registrations granted were outside of the permissible circumstances outlined in the Federal Insecticide, Fungicide, and Rodenticide Act (FIFRA). The results of this analysis were included in an OPP internal review report and posted on OPP's website.

To address the second objective—the extent to which EPA ensures that registrants submit the additional data required as part of conditional

---

[5]These key changes followed implementation of the Food Quality Protection Act of 1996.

registrations and reviews these data—we interviewed OPP officials about how they manage conditional registration data requirements. We also asked OPP to provide information on the number of pesticides that (1) have a conditional registration, but the registrant has not submitted the additional required data by the specified due date; (2) have a conditional registration and the registrant has submitted the additional required data, but EPA has not reviewed these data; (3) still have a conditional registration, even though the registrant has submitted, and EPA has reviewed, the additional required data; and (4) had been changed from conditional to unconditional status. However, OPP officials said they could not provide these data because they do not have an automated data system that tracks this information, but that they did analyze a subset of 544 conditional registrations to try to determine whether registrants had submitted the required data and posted the results of this analysis on OPP's website.

To obtain the views of relevant stakeholders on EPA's conditional registration process and ways, if any to improve it, we administered a questionnaire to 35 professionals in the consumer, environmental, industry, legal, producer, science, and state government fields. We used a multistage process to identify our final nonprobability sample of 35 potential respondents.[6] This process included (1) conducting a literature search to identify groups or individuals who had recently published articles on registration (including conditional registration) of pesticides, (2) asking agency and other relevant officials for recommendations of knowledgeable parties in each of these areas, and (3) asking prospective stakeholders for suggestions of other potential stakeholders. Through these methods, we arrived at an initial list of 148 potential stakeholders that were divided, based on their institutional affiliation, into the seven categories listed above. We then narrowed this list by (1) performing online searches of the professional affiliations of each stakeholder to determine whether they would likely have sufficient knowledge about EPA's conditional registration of pesticides and (2) conducting screening interviews, by phone and e-mail, to determine whether the individuals were sufficiently familiar with EPA's process for registering pesticides and

---

[6]Because this was a nonprobability sample, the information collected in response to the questionnaire about EPA's use of conditional registrations cannot be generalized to all consumer, environmental, industry, legal, producer, science, and state government stakeholders but provides illustrative information on the views of such stakeholders by category.

to secure their commitment to participate in our survey. After this process
was completed, we arrived at a list of 35 stakeholders to whom we sent,
via e-mail, our questionnaire.

The questionnaire asked about, among other things, (1) problems, if any,
associated with each of the permissible situations for which registrations
can be conditionally granted; (2) risks, if any, associated with registrants
not submitting data required by a conditional registration in a timely
manner; (3) pesticides with conditional registrations that stakeholders
believe should not have been conditionally registered; and (4)
suggestions for improving EPA's conditional registration process. In
preparing to administer this questionnaire, we conducted three pretests to
ensure that the questions were clear, terminology was used appropriately,
and the questionnaire was unbiased. We used the results of our pretests
to revise the questions as needed. The questions were open-ended, and
thus issues raised by stakeholders had to be "volunteered." We did not
ask each stakeholder to agree or disagree with particular issues.

The administration period for this questionnaire was from July through
September 2012. Of the 35 participating stakeholders, 24 provided
complete, valid questionnaire responses.[7] The organizations that
participated as stakeholders were Akin Gump, LLP; American Chemistry
Council; American Farm Bureau Federation; Beyond Pesticides;
California Department of Pesticide Regulation; Center for Biological
Diversity; Center for Environmental Health; Center for Food Safety;
Center for Science in the Public Interest; Council of Producers and
Distributors of Agrotechnology; CropLife America; Dow Agrosciences,
LLC; Earthjustice; Environmental Working Group; Food and Water Watch;
Florida Department of Agriculture and Consumer Services; Iowa
Department of Agriculture; McDermott, Will and Emery, LLP; Natural
Resources Defense Council; New York State Department of
Environmental Conservation; Pesticide Action Network North America;
Syngenta Crop Protection, LLC; Texas Department of Agriculture; and
The Endocrine Disruption Exchange. The results of this questionnaire
cannot be generalized to all parties knowledgeable about the conditional
registration of pesticides; rather our analysis of the results of this

---

[7]Seven stakeholders did not respond to our request to complete the questionnaire.
Although three stakeholders provided complete responses, we did not consider them valid
because they responded as individuals instead of as representatives of their respective
organizations. Another stakeholder declined to fill out the questionnaire.

questionnaire identifies common themes present in the responses of
those who participated in our questionnaire.

We analyzed stakeholder responses to the questionnaire to identify
themes and develop summary findings. Two GAO analysts separately
conducted this analysis and placed users' responses into one or more
categories, then compared these analyses. All initial disagreements
regarding the categorizations of stakeholders' responses were discussed
and reconciled. The analysts then tallied the number of responses in each
category.

We conducted this performance audit from September 2011 to August
2013 in accordance with generally accepted government auditing
standards. Those standards require that we plan and perform the audit to
obtain sufficient, appropriate evidence to provide a reasonable basis for
our findings and conclusions based on our audit objectives. We believe
that the evidence obtained provides a reasonable basis for our findings
and conclusions based on our audit objectives.

Appendix II: Comments from the Environmental Protection Agency

UNITED STATES ENVIRONMENTAL PROTECTION AGENCY
WASHINGTON, D.C. 20460

JUL 1 8 2013

OFFICE OF CHEMICAL SAFETY
AND POLLUTION PREVENTION

Mr. Alfredo Gomez
Acting Director
Natural Resources and Environment
U.S. Government Accountability Office
Washington, DC 20548

Dear Mr. Gomez:

Thank you for the opportunity to review and comment on the Government Accountability Office's (GAO) draft report entitled *Pesticides: EPA Should Take Steps to Improve its Oversight of Conditional Registrations* (GAO-13-145). GAO stated as its objectives for this evaluation to answer the following questions:

1. For the period FY 1996 through 2011, how many conditional registrations for pesticide products were granted by EPA and on what basis were these granted?
2. How does EPA ensure that registrants meet requirements for removing the conditional status of pesticide product registrations, what actions does the agency take when these requirements are not met, and how many conditional registrations has EPA changed to unconditional when the requirements were met?
3. What are the views of environmental, public health, consumer, industry, academic and other stakeholders on EPA's use of conditional registrations and ways, if any, to improve EPA's conditional registration process?

The EPA appreciates GAO's effort in evaluating the legal, scientific and data management issues involving the conditional registration of pesticides. The EPA acknowledges that the agency has made mistakes in how it has identified the status of conditionally and unconditionally registered pesticides in its records and that its computerized record-keeping system has significant limitations. Nonetheless, the EPA believes that, despite these challenges, all conditionally registered products meet applicable legal standards, and pesticides have not been allowed in the marketplace without adequate testing to ensure safety to both human health and the environment.

Background

Before responding to the specific recommendations, it is useful to review briefly the history and purpose of conditional pesticide registrations. In 1972, Congress established a new standard for the registration of pesticides -- EPA could register a pesticide only if the agency had sufficient data to show the pesticide would not cause "unreasonable adverse effects on the environment." After this standard was added, EPA could not register any new pesticides unless applications provided all the information required under then-current scientific standards. Because scientific standards had become more rigorous after the time that many pesticide products were initially

1

registered, EPA required that the applicants seeking registration of new pesticide products provide significantly more data than had been required in the past. This led to a paradoxical situation. EPA would deny registration to a new product that was identical to a currently registered product on the grounds that EPA lacked the data necessary to conclude that the new product met the "unreasonable adverse effects on the environment" standard, even though the identical product was still allowed to be sold and used.

To remedy the unfairness of this situation, in 1978, Congress gave EPA the authority to register a pesticide product "conditionally" if it was identical or substantially similar to a currently registered product, despite the fact that there were gaps in the data needed to determine whether the pesticide would cause unreasonable adverse effects on the environment.

Before granting a conditional registration for such a product, EPA must determine that, although the application lacks some of the necessary data, registration would not significantly increase the risk of unreasonable adverse effects on the environment.[1] Congress also recognized that it would be appropriate to give EPA discretionary authority, in very narrow circumstances, to approve the registration of a product containing a new active ingredient for which EPA requires additional data.[2] To approve the conditional registration of a new active ingredient, EPA must determine that:

1. The missing data were required so recently that the applicant would not have had time to generate the studies;
2. The pesticide would meet the safety standard during the time needed to generate the necessary data; and
3. The registration would be in the public interest.

In these circumstances, the registrant typically has from 1-4 years to provide the missing data, depending on the type of study to be submitted. Subsequently, after reviewing these new data, EPA may pursue changes to the registration if the new data raise concerns.

Under FIFRA, the status of a product as conditionally or unconditionally registered does not affect the ability of registrants or others to sell, distribute, or use the products. The main difference between a conditionally and an unconditionally registered pesticide concerns the obligation on the registrant of a conditionally registered product to provide data required at the time of the initial registration. Finally, there is no legal duty on EPA to convert a conditional registration to an unconditional registration once the registrant of a conditionally registered pesticide has met the condition to provide additional data, and doing so would have no practical impact on anyone selling or using the pesticide.

Data Supporting Conditional Registrations

In September 2010, EPA's Office of Pesticide Programs (OPP) initiated an internal review of its conditional registration program. The review focused in part on the following key questions:

1. Did registrants of pesticides conditionally registered submit the required data;
2. Did EPA review the submitted data; and

---

[1] See FIFRA section 3(c)(7)(A) or (B).
[2] See FIFRA section 3(c)(7)(C).

2

3. Did the data reviews lead OPP to seek regulatory changes in the terms of the registration?

Based on the review's findings, EPA began to implement changes and voluntarily issued a report on its website providing information on its review and steps it would take to address certain issues.

For this review, OPP examined a subset of recent registrations (from 2000 -2010) to ascertain if the data had been submitted and reviewed. Because its database does not contain the type of information that would allow OPP to determine if registrants had met the data submission requirements imposed when EPA issued the conditional registration, EPA examined the paper records associated with these registrations. This "hard-copy" analysis showed that registrants had in fact submitted data for 533 of the 544 conditionally registered pesticides (98%). The analysis also showed that EPA had reviewed this data for 523 of the 533 submissions (98%). The analysis concluded that for 96 % of these registrations, all actions required by the conditional registration had been completed in a timely fashion. In addition, OPP's review of the data supporting the conditional registrations examined in this analysis did not lead us to believe that any change was required in either the initial risk assessment or the risk management decision supporting any labeled product. Overall, the analysis of the data supported EPA's findings at the time of the initial product registration; in other words, that the pesticides were properly reviewed and labeled, and that the products continued to be safe.

Tracking Conditional Registrations

The internal review also looked at the use of the term "conditional registration" in the program, the computer coding associated with conditional registrations, and the potential for improvements to tracking these registrations. The review showed that many of the pesticide products in OPP's data system were incorrectly identified, and erroneously coded as conditional registrations. Although they were coded as conditional registrations, the products still met the safety standard for registration. As discussed below, EPA is implementing a plan to change the recordkeeping to improve clarity.

EPA Response to GAO Recommendations

EPA agrees with the three recommendations in GAO's draft report. As GAO noted in its report, OPP has actions underway to more accurately account for conditional registrations. Listed below are the GAO's recommendations, followed by the EPA efforts underway to implement each recommendation.

1. Complete plans to automate data related to conditional registrations to more readily track the status of these registrations and related registrant and agency actions and identify potential problems requiring management attention.

OPP's implementation plan to automate data related to conditional registrations includes the following key elements:

- Development of new codes for identifying conditional registration decisions in the computerized registration tracking system (OPPIN); and
- Changes to its databases to allow staff to check more easily whether there are any outstanding requests for data on any pesticide active ingredients.

3

OPP has provided training to its staff on use of the new categories represented by the new conditional registration codes, and will make the training available on-line for guidance.

Depending on funding and the complexity of incorporating changes to the databases, OPP plans to develop a more comprehensive system for tracking conditional registrations.

2. Pending development of an automated data system for tracking the status of conditional registrations, develop guidance to ensure that product managers use a uniform methodology to track and document this information, including when data are submitted by registrants and reviewed by EPA, in the files maintained by each pesticide product manager.

OPP is developing a standard operating procedure (SOP) for staff to follow when entering data in the computerized tracking system about the statutory basis for registration decisions. This SOP, together with the new training of staff, should ensure that conditional registration decisions are properly identified in the OPPIN database going forward. We expect to complete the SOP this calendar year. OPP is also reviewing and updating the status of products previously approved under the conditional registration authority, as necessary.

3. Review and correct, as appropriate, OPP's website on conditional registrations to ensure that the information presented is clear, concise, and accurate, including defining technical terms.

OPP will revise its website on conditional registration to both clarify and update the information presented. We expect to complete revision of the website by the end of the year. The website will include an outline of ongoing agency work to strengthen its conditional pesticide registration program.

Overall, we are pleased that the GAO draft report recognizes EPA's continuing efforts to improve the management and tracking of conditional registrations. EPA is also submitting a separate document with specific technical comments on the draft report.

Sincerely,

James J. Jones
Acting Assistant Administrator

Enclosure: Technical Comments
cc: EPA GAO Liaison Team

4

Appendix III: GAO Contact and Staff Acknowledgments

GAO Contact	J. Alfredo Gómez, (202) 512-3841 or gomezj@gao.gov
Staff Acknowledgments	In addition to the individual named above, James R. Jones, Jr., Assistant Director; Jameal Addison; Kevin Bray; Kirsten B. Lauber; Robin Marion; Lisa Shames; Carol Herrnstadt Shulman; Kathryn Smith; and Lisa Turner made key contributions to this report. Colleen M. Candrl, Joyce Evans, Dan Royer, and Kiki Theodoropoulos also made important contributions to this report.

Related GAO Products

Nanotechnology: Improved Performance Information Needed for Environmental, Health, and Safety Research. GAO-12-427. Washington, D.C.: May 21, 2012.

Agricultural Chemicals: USDA Could Enhance Pesticide and Fertilizer Usage Data, Improve Outreach, and Better Leverage Resources. GAO-11-37. Washington, D.C.: November 4, 2010.

Pesticides on Tobacco: Federal Activities to Assess Risks and Monitor Residues. GAO-03-485. Washington, D.C.: March 26, 2003.

Agricultural Pesticides: Management Improvements Needed to Further Promote Integrated Pest Management. GAO-01-815. Washington, D.C.: August 17, 2001.

Children and Pesticides: New Approach to Considering Risk is Partly in Place. GAO/HEHS-00-175. Washington, D.C.: September 11, 2000.

Pesticides: Improvements Needed to Ensure the Safety of Farmworkers and Their Children. GAO/RCED-00-40. Washington, D.C.: March 14, 2000.

GAO Products Related to Pesticide Regulation. GAO/RCED-95-272R. Washington, D.C.: September 26, 1995.

Pesticides: Information Systems Improvements Essential for EPA's Reregistration Efforts. GAO/IMTEC-93-5. Washington, D.C.: November 23, 1992.

Pesticides: EPA's Information Systems Provide Inadequate Support for Reregistration. GAO/T-IMTEC-92-3. Washington, D.C.: October 30, 1991.

Pesticides: EPA's Formidable Task to Assess and Regulate Their Risks. GAO/RCED-86-125. Washington, D.C.: April 18, 1986.

Natural Resources and Environment: Delays and Unresolved Issues Plague New Pesticide Protection Programs. GAO/CED-80-32. Washington, D.C.: February 15, 1980.

GAO's Mission	The Government Accountability Office, the audit, evaluation, and investigative arm of Congress, exists to support Congress in meeting its constitutional responsibilities and to help improve the performance and accountability of the federal government for the American people. GAO examines the use of public funds; evaluates federal programs and policies; and provides analyses, recommendations, and other assistance to help Congress make informed oversight, policy, and funding decisions. GAO's commitment to good government is reflected in its core values of accountability, integrity, and reliability.
Obtaining Copies of GAO Reports and Testimony	The fastest and easiest way to obtain copies of GAO documents at no cost is through GAO's website (http://www.gao.gov). Each weekday afternoon, GAO posts on its website newly released reports, testimony, and correspondence. To have GAO e-mail you a list of newly posted products, go to http://www.gao.gov and select "E-mail Updates."
Order by Phone	The price of each GAO publication reflects GAO's actual cost of production and distribution and depends on the number of pages in the publication and whether the publication is printed in color or black and white. Pricing and ordering information is posted on GAO's website, http://www.gao.gov/ordering.htm. Place orders by calling (202) 512-6000, toll free (866) 801-7077, or TDD (202) 512-2537. Orders may be paid for using American Express, Discover Card, MasterCard, Visa, check, or money order. Call for additional information.
Connect with GAO	Connect with GAO on Facebook, Flickr, Twitter, and YouTube. Subscribe to our RSS Feeds or E-mail Updates. Listen to our Podcasts. Visit GAO on the web at www.gao.gov.
To Report Fraud, Waste, and Abuse in Federal Programs	Contact: Website: http://www.gao.gov/fraudnet/fraudnet.htm E-mail: fraudnet@gao.gov Automated answering system: (800) 424-5454 or (202) 512-7470
Congressional Relations	Katherine Siggerud, Managing Director, siggerudk@gao.gov, (202) 512-4400, U.S. Government Accountability Office, 441 G Street NW, Room 7125, Washington, DC 20548
Public Affairs	Chuck Young, Managing Director, youngc1@gao.gov, (202) 512-4800 U.S. Government Accountability Office, 441 G Street NW, Room 7149 Washington, DC 20548

Please Print on Recycled Paper.